Ledia DUSHI

Rain in the Dark

Translated from the Albanian by Robert Elsie

TRANSCENDENT ZERO PRESS

HOUSTON, TEXAS

PUBLISHED BY TRANSCENDENT ZERO PRESS
www.transcendentzeropress.org

ISBN-13: 978-1-946460-11-0

Printed in the United States of America

Transcendent Zero Press
16429 El Camino Real Apt. #7
Houston, TX 77062

Cover image from https://www.pexels.com/photo/butterfly-leaf-rain-drop-605733/

FIRST EDITION

Ledia DUSHI

Rain in the Dark

Translated from the Albanian by Robert Elsie

FREEDOM AND CHAOS
CONTEMPORARY ALBANIAN LITERATURE
Robert Elsie

Never in Albanian history have there been so many books on the market and never has so much Albanian literature, prose, poetry and other genres, been produced and published. Never has freedom of thought and creativity reigned throughout the Albanian world as it does today. And yet, it is often said that Albanian literature still finds itself in an age of profound crisis, of loss of identity and of disintegration.

From the 1980s, when I first started to take an interest in Albanian literature, and up until the end of the 20th century, it was always possible to keep abreast of Albanian-language publications, to know what had been published, virtually every book, and to know what Albanian intellectuals thought of the works and authors in question.

The Stalinist dictatorship imploded in 1991 and the Albanians, after forty-five years of total isolation from the rest of the world, as if they had been living on a different planet, found themselves robbed of any chance they might have had at keeping up with the rest of Europe. In material terms, they had been deprived of all but the barest essentials needed to stay alive.

It is difficult for the foreign observer to appreciate what the people of Albania went through when the only world they knew, i.e. the awesome political system set up by the communist aristocracy, and the economy and social order which arose with it, collapsed and was initially replaced by... nothing. For writers and intellectuals it was a period of relief, of joy and of apprehension. Freedom had finally dawned, but no one really knew what freedom was. Rumours spread in the early nineties that ships laden with gold and riches would appear on the horizon and that little Albania would be transformed overnight into a 'second Switzerland,' the country it would allegedly have been from the start, had Enver Hoxha not refused so stubbornly to shake hands with the West. Others literally took to the ships themselves, believing that they would be welcomed in Italy with open arms after having suffered so many years of oppression and horror. The little prisons in that big prison which was Albania were opened, and political prisoners resurfaced in the cities. Among them were many talented writers, old before their time and broken after fifteen to forty years in the concentration camps of Spaç, Qafë-Bari and Burrel, or in the dreary internment villages on the mosquito-infested plains of Myzeqe. But their tales were of a bygone age. Everyone was too busy merely surviving.

As the country's socialist economy collapsed like a little matchstick house, so too did the modest institutions of Albanian culture: the state publishing companies, the Writers' Union and the national theatres. Funding for libraries, concert halls, theatres and higher education vanished overnight.

By the mid-nineties, new private structures, at least for printing, had been put in place and Albanian literature was once again being published and marketed, though still under very primitive and chaotic conditions. Books in Albania were sold in the same manner as soap and other commodities. Young men, otherwise unemployed, arrived in Tirana by bus in the morning and returned to their provincial hometowns in the late afternoon with sacks of books, which were hawked on the muddy sidewalks. Such were the distribution structures of the publishing industry in Albania until quite recently. Even in the nation's capital, more books were sold on overturned cardboard boxes in the streets and in improvised kiosks than in the bookstores themselves.

Publishers were understandably interested in a quick profit and demanded cash in advance for the publication of a book, any book. There were no more editors and no more revisions of texts before publication. After decades of total regulation in the publishing industry, there were no controls on books in the nineties at all. Anyone who had money or a sponsor could publish and market whatever he or she wished. The result for the reading public was mistrust and disorientation, and a growing suspicion that Albanian writers could produce nothing of sustainable value.

Most foreign literature, and virtually all contemporary foreign works devoid of a Marxist message, had been banned, or at least were not available under the dictatorship. It is understandable, therefore, that Albanian readers in the nineties and in this century have been much more interested in translations of foreign literature than they have been in books originally written in Albanian. The truth of the matter is that, with the exception of the works of Ismail Kadare, few Albanian novels published in Tirana in recent years have sold more than 100 copies.

Surprisingly enough, though quality control has been nonexistent and interest in new works of Albanian literature has fallen dramatically, the quantity of books published in Albanian over the last five years has risen substantially. Bookstores are better stocked than ever before, at least in Tirana.

One phenomenon which has had an extremely negative impact on Albanian society and culture in recent years has been mass emigration. After the collapse of the Albanian State in March 1997 following the implosion of the pyramid investment schemes and the plundering of military installations and arms depots, many young people came to believe that they had no future in their country. Hardship and deprivation have always been part of life in Albania, but patience by then had come to an end. By the close of the century, the vast majority of writers and intellectuals, young and old, had indeed left Albania in search of a better life abroad. Few will ever return.

The early nineties also marked a turning point for the Albanians of Kosova and Macedonia. The communist system in Yugoslavia had collapsed, and so had Yugoslavia. The Albanians in Kosova, now under harsh Serb rule, were faced with an appalling form of discrimination, that of ethnic persecution, which led ultimately to ethnic cleansing. Politically, the country found itself in a downward spiral which led inevitably to the 1999 war, but also to final liberation after so many years of torment.

Writers in Kosova, as opposed to their counterparts in Albania itself, had no desire or intention to leave their country. They were solidly committed to building a new nation. By the second half of the nineties, the political and economic situation in Kosova had, however, become so untenable that many writers had no choice but to flee the country or suffer imprisonment... or indeed be murdered by the State in which they lived.

Literature, nonetheless, continued to be published in Prishtina, even in the darkest hours of Yugoslav rule. For the Albanians, books were an act of resistance to Serbian cultural hegemony. The Serbs themselves, who had been taught to despise the Albanians as an 'inferior race,' regarded the very thought of creative literature in Albanian as ridiculous. As such, once Belgrade had lost its political authority over the Kosova Albanians, it had no more opportunity, and probably no particular interest, in banning or censoring Albanian books. literature in Kosova. With Belgrade's illegal takeover and liquidation of the state-owned Rilindja Publishing Company, quality controls in publishing, however, disappeared, as they had in Albania. But books in fact did continue to circulate. Draped over the hoods of cars on street corners, they were hawked throughout Kosova in an impromptu manner. All traces of them could be removed instantly if the Serb police did decide to intervene. The Kosova Albanians were proud of every one of the books, although fewof the latter were actually read.

In addition to the consequences of political developments up to the summer of 1997, there are two other factors which had a negative influence on the development of creative literature in Kosova. Firstly, the standard literary language, gjuha letrare, more akin to the southern Albanian Tosk dialect, is quite different from the language spoken in Kosova. Having been deprived by the Belgrade authorities of an Albanian-language public education system for a whole generation, many young Kosova authors now have trouble expressing themselves in standard Albanian with requisite literary refinement. Secondly, after years of ethnic strife and oppression, many works of Kosova literature are understandably pervaded in one form or another by a strong sense of Albanian identity. Although a nationalist perspective does not necessarily preclude good literature, it is an ideological framework which, at the end of the day, proves to be just as constrictive of free creative thought as any other political or religious ideology. Many readers from Albania, at any rate, seem to have difficulties appreciating literature from Kosova.

Such has been the environment in which Albanian literature has evolved over the last fifteen years, since the fall of the Communist dictatorship. I would like now to review some of what I regard as the major achievements of Albanian literary culture in this period, beginning perhaps traditionally, but also quite justifiably with Albania's best known writer, Ismail Kadare.

Ismail Kadare (b. 1936) is and, without a doubt, remains the best example of creativity and originality in contemporary Albanian letters. He is, in addition, the only Albanian writer to enjoy a broad international reputation. Kadare's talents have lost none of their innovative force over the last four decades. His courage in attacking literary mediocrity within the communist system brought a breath of fresh air to Albanian culture in the sombre years of imposed conformity.

Ismail Kadare began his literary career in Albania with poetry but turned increasingly to prose, of which he soon became the undisputed master and by far the most popular writer of the whole of Albanian literature. His works were extremely influential throughout the 1970s and 1980s and, for many readers, he was the only ray of hope in the chilly, dismal prison that was communist Albania. Ismail Kadare lived the next thirty years of his life in Tirana, constantly under the Damocles Sword of the Party. He was privileged by the authorities, in particular once his works became known internationally. Indeed, he was able to pursue literary and personal objectives for which other writers would certainly have been sent into internal exile or to prison. But Kadare knew well that liberties in Albania could be withdrawn easily, by an impulsive stroke of the tyrant's quill. At the end of October 1990, a mere two months before the final collapse of the dictatorship, Ismail Kadare left Tirana and applied for political asylum in France. His departure enabled him for the first time to exercise his profession with complete freedom. His years of Parisian exile were productive and accorded him further success and recognition, as a writer both in Albanian and in French. After twelve years in Paris, he returned to Tirana in 2002.

Though Kadare is still admired as a poet in Albania, his reputation and, in particular, his international reputation now rest entirely upon his prose, especially his historical novels. Of his literary works translated into English, mention may be made of the following: *The General of the Dead Army*, London 1971 (Gjenerali i ushtrisë së vdekur, Tirana 1963); *Chronicle in Stone*, New York & London 1987 (Kronikë në gur, Tirana 1971); Doruntine, New York & London 1988 (Kush e solli Doruntinën? 1979); *Broken April*, New York & London 1990 (Prilli i thyer, 1978); *The Palace of Dreams*, New York & London 1993 (Nëpunësi i pallatit të ëndrrave, 1981); *The Concert*, New York & London 1994 (Koncert në fund të dimrit, Tirana 1988); *The Pyramid*, New York & London 1996 (Piramida, 1993); *The File on H*, New York & London 1997 (Dosja H, Tirana 1990); *The Three-Arched Bridge*, New York 1997 & London 1998 (Ura me tri harqe, Tirana 1978); *The Wedding Procession Turned to Ice*, Boulder 1997 (Krushqit janë të ngrirë, 1986); *Three Elegies for Kosovo*, London 2000 (Tri këngë zie për Kosovën, Tirana 1998), also called *Elegy for Kosovo* New York 2000; and *Spring Flowers, Spring Frost*, New York 2002 (Lulet e ftohta të marsit, Tirana 2000). Of the above twelve works, only five (*Chronicle in Stone, Broken April, The Three-Arched Bridge, The Wedding Procession Turned to Ice*, and *Three Elegies for Kosovo*) were translated directly from the Albanian. All the others were translated from the French-language versions by Jusuf Vrioni (1916-2001). I am excluding here early, very stilted translations of *The Wedding*, Tirana 1968 (Dasma, Tirana 1968) and *The Castle*, Tirana 1974 (Kështjella, Tirana 1970), which fortunately never circulated much in the West. Ismail Kadare has lost none of his elan in recent years.

In addition to some works of a journalistic and political nature, he has published the short story collection *Përballë pasqyrës së një gruaje,* Tirana 2001 (*In a lady's looking-glass*); the novel *Jeta, loja dhe vdekja e Lul Mazrekut,* Tirana 2002 (*Life, game and death of Lul Mazreku*); a play, the Promethean tragedy *Stinë e mërzitshme në Olymp,* Tirana 2002 (*Boring season on Olympus*); the poetry collections *Ca pika shiu ranë mbi qelq,* Tirana 2003 (*Some raindrops fell on the window-pane*) and *Kristal,* Tirana 2004 (*Crystal*), both essentially republications; and the novels Pasardhësi, Tirana 2003 (*The Successor*) and *Vajza e Agamemnonit,* Tïrana 2003 (*Agamemnon's daughter*).

Ismail Kadare has also recently published his collected works in twelve thick volumes, each in an Albanian-language and a French-language edition, and has been given membership in the prestigious Académie Française (28 October 1996) and in the French Legion of Honour. He has also been nominated on several occasions for the Nobel Prize for Literature.

There can be no doubt that Ismail Kadare was a profoundly dissident writer who, at the same time, led an extremely conformist, if you will, collaborationist life. Dissent in Kadare's prose up to the fall of the dictatorship was very discreet but ubiquitous. Notwithstanding its subtle nature, it was sufficiently evident at all times to the educated Albanian reader, and this is one of the major factors which contributed to his popularity at home. Kadare left no opportunity untouched to attack the follies, weaknesses and excesses of the Albanian communist system, yet many of his subtle barbs are difficult to grasp for those who did not grow up in or live through that system. The very treatment in a conformist manner of a taboo subject, i.e., of virtually anything beyond the very narrow scope of socialist realism and communist partisan heroism, constituted in itself an act of extreme dissent, amounting to treason in Albania. Though some observers in Albania silently viewed him as a political opportunist, and many Albanians in exile later criticized him vociferously for the compromises he made, it is Ismail Kadare more than anyone else who, from within the system, dealt the death blow to the literature of socialist realism. There can be no doubt that he made use of his relative freedom and his talent under the dictatorship to launch many a subtle but effective fusillade against the regime in the form of political allegories which occur throughout his works. Ismail Kadare was thus the most prominent representative of Albanian literature under the dictatorship of Enver Hoxha (1908-1985) and, at the same time, the regime's most talented adversary.

Kadare's international renown has cast a bit of a shadow over all other Albanian writers, yet there are many others who are worthy of the limelight. One writer who has had a far from negligible influence on the course of contemporary literature is **Dritëro Agolli** (b. 1931), who was head of the Albanian Union of Writers and Artists from the purge of Fadil Paçrami and Todi Lubonja at the Fourth Plenary Session in 1973 until 1992. Agolli was born to a peasant family in Menkulas in the Devoll region near Korça and finished secondary school in Gjirokastra in 1952. He later continued his studies at the Faculty of Arts of the University of Leningrad and took up journalism upon his return to Albania, working for the daily newspaper *Zëri i Popullit* (The People's Voice) for fifteen years. Agolli not only served as president of the Writers' Union from 1973 to his retirement on 31 January 1992, but was also a deputy in the People's Assembly.

Like Kadare, Dritëro Agolli turned increasingly to prose in the seventies after attaining success as a poet of the soil. He first made a name for himself with the novel *Komisari Memo*, Tirana 1970 (Commissar Memo), originally conceived as a short story. This didactic novel with a clear social and political message was translated into English as *The Bronze bust*, Tirana 1975. Agolli's second novel, *Njeriu me top*, Tirana 1975 (The Man with a cannon), translated into English as *The Man with the gun*, Tirana 1983, takes up the partisan theme from a different angle and with a somewhat more subtle approach. After these two rather conformist novels of partisan heroism, the standard theme encouraged by the party, Agolli produced a far more interesting work, his satirical *Shkëlqimi dhe rënja e shokut* Zylo, Tirana 1973 (The Splendour and fall of comrade Zylo), which is unfortunately not available in English, yet which has proved to be his claim to fame. Comrade Zylo is the epitome of the well-meaning but incompetent apparatchik, director of an obscure government cultural affairs department. His pathetic vanity, his quixotic fervour, his grotesque public behaviour, in short his splendour and fall, are all recorded in ironic detail by his hardworking and more astute subordinate and friend Demkë who serves as a neutral observer. 'The Splendour and Fall of Comrade Zylo' first appeared in 1972 in the Tirana satirical journal *Hostenl* (The Goad) and was published the following year in book form. That it was published at all in Stalinist Albania is linked to the fact that the character of Zylo was modelled on a well known liberal journalist and writer of the time and thus served to discredit the so-called liberal movement in general.

All in all, Agolli's strength in prose lies in the short story rather than in the novel. Sixteen of his short stories were published in English in the volume: Short stories, Tirana 1985. Though he was a leading figure in the communist nomenclature, he remained a highly respected figure of public and literary life after the fall of the dictatorship, and is still one the most widely read authors in Albania. In the early 1990s, he was active for several years as a member of parliament for the now ruling Socialist Party of Albania. He also founded his own Dritëro Publishing Company by means of which he has been able to publish many new volumes of prose and poetry, and make an impact on literary and intellectual life in the country. Among recent volumes of prose are: the short story collection *Njerëz të krisur*, Tirana 1995 (Insane people); the novels *Kalorësi lakuriq*, Tirana 1996 (The Naked horseman); and in particular the volume *Arka e djallit*, Tirana 1997 (The Devil's box). Dritëro Agolli was a prolific writer throughout the nineties, a rare voice of humanity and sincerity in Albanian letters.

Prose author **Fatos Kongoli** (b. 1944) has recently become one of the most forceful and convincing representatives of contemporary Albanian literature. He was born and raised in Elbasan and studied mathematics in China during the tense years of the Sino-Albanian alliance. Kongoli chose not to publish any major works during the dictatorship. Rather than this, he devoted his creative energies at the time to an obscure and apolitical career as a mathematician, and waited for the storm to pass. His narrative talent and individual style only really emerged, at any rate, in the nineties, since the fall of the communist dictatorship.

Fatos Kongoli's first major novel, *I humburi*, Tirana 1992 (The Loser), is set in March 1991, when over 10,000 refugees scrambled onto a decrepit and heavily rusting freighter to escape the past and to reach the marvellous West. There they washed up, unwanted, on the shores of southern Italy. At the last moment before setting sail, protagonist Thesar Lumi, the 'loser' for whom all hope is too late, abandons his companions, disembarks and walks home. "I returned to my neighbourhood at the fall of night. No one had seen me leave and no one saw me come back." The narrative of the novel returns at this point to the long and numbing years of the Hoxha dictatorship to revive the climate of terror and universal despair which characterized day-to-day life in Albania in the sixties and seventies. Thesar Lumi was born on the banks of a river (Alb. lumi) in the looming shadow of the people's own cement factory, which produced more dust than it ever did cement. Despite a skeleton in the family closet, an uncle who had earlier fled the country, Thesar manages to get himself registered at the university, and penetrates briefly into a milieu which is not his own and never will be, that of the ruling families of Albania's red aristocracy. "At a tender age I learned that I belonged to an inferior race or, as I saw things at the time, to a category of mangy dogs to be kicked about and chased away." Thesar, whose fate in Albania's hermetic and suffocating society has been sealed once and for all, returns to live a life of futility and despair in a universe with no heroes. Far from the active protagonist struggling to control of his own destiny or even from the staid positive hero of socialist realism, Thesar Lumi is incapable of action and incapable of living. He is the voice of all the 'losers' who glimpse the silver clouds on the horizon and know full well that they will never reach them. "My existence is that of the mediocre, setting out from nothing and going nowhere." When first published in 1992, in what was a comparatively large edition of 10,000 copies, the novel found immediate success among the reading public. Who could not identify with the confessional monologue and the unending tribulations and torment of Thesar Lumi?

Kongoli's second novel, *Kufoma*, Tirana 1994 (The Corpse), has clear affinities with its predecessor, both with respect to Kongoli's now crystallized and somewhat more elaborate narrative style, and to his innate preoccupations. Protagonist Festim Gurabardhi is another loser, caught up in the inhumane machinery of the last decade of the Stalinist dictatorship in Albania. As an orphan in the fifties he could never understand why his parents, killed in a car crash eight months after his birth, had given him the name Festim, meaning 'feast, celebration.' What was there to celebrate? "My childhood was endless solitude in boarding-schools, refectories and dormitories which made the solitary souls in them even lonelier." He observes his playmates slitting the throats of cats in the street, observes his brother Abel being arrested and taken away in a sinister black limousine, and then, as an adult employed at the state-run publishing company, he observes himself ... being observed. The communist dictatorship in Albania was the perfection of insanity. What the country produced more than anything was paranoia and schizophrenia. Intellectual life in Albania, or what remained of it after the countless arrests, purges and suicides, was concentrated in the Tirana publishing companies. There, under the thumb of boorish directors and under the constant observation of spies and submissive apparatchiks, the nation's traumatized writers and translators were assembled to edit the sage works of the supreme leader and other members of the politburo. Like the characters of an ancient tragedy, they had resigned themselves to their fates and capitulated, emotionally and intellectually. In the macabre and Kafkaesque game of cats and mice which Kongoli portrays, Festim and his colleagues are destined to play both roles, that of the victim and that of the perpetrator. The metaphorical background is grey and realistic, depressing even for those who knew Albania at the time: the sombre and filthy hallways, the furtive drunkenness, sordid copulation in the director's office, and the eternal stench of the rat-infested toilets. Fatos Kongoli is at his best in portraying this very atmosphere, in providing a detailed autopsy of an unending nightmare.

Kongoli's *Dragoi i fildishtë*, Tirana 1999 (The Ivory dragon), focusses primarily on the life of an Albanian student in China in the 1960s. For Genc Skampa and the other fictive Albanian students highlighted in the novel, studies in China provided an opportunity to discover the world. Having contact not only with their Chinese comrades but also with foreign students from all over the globe. they were able to pursue their goals of intellectual and personal development. Among these pursuits were discreet sexual freedoms which would have been unthinkable in puritanical Albania itself, where everyone was watching everyone with a malevolent eye. Interwoven into the novel is the life of the protagonist in post-communist Albania thirty years later when, as a journalist, he is invited to Paris with a group of Balkan colleagues. Now divorced and suffering from personal isolation and the ravages of alcohol, he looks back in a haze to the decisive years of his life in China and ponders over the emotional consequences of his turbulent love affair with Sui Lin. 'The Ivory dragon' is the tragic parable of one man's life, of adventure, alienation and self-destruction. Although the backdrop to this novel is quite different from the earlier works, the underlying themes of despair and isolation are the same.

Most successful and most elaborate of all would seem to be Kongoli's fourth novel in the tetralogy, *Lëkura e qenit*, Tirana 2003 (The Dog's skin) which has just been published in Slovak and is currently being translated into French and German. Of other modern prose authors, mention may be made of **Luan Starova** (b. 1941) of Skopje, whose novels have been translated into French and German; **Musa Ramadani** (b. 1944) from Gjilan; the late **Beqir Musliu** (1945-1996) from Gjilan; **Zija Çela** (b. 1946) of Shkodra; Jusuf Buxhovi (b. 1946) of Peja; **Eqrem Basha** (b. 1948) from Dibra, whose short story collection *Marshi i kërmillit*, Peja 1994 (The Snail's march), and the recent novel *Dyert e heshtjes*, Peja 2001 (The Gates of silence), have been well received; **Sabri Hamiti** (b. 1950) of Podujeva, also a leading and innovative literary critic, poet and playwright; **Ylljet Aliçka** (b. 1951) from Tirana, whose works, in particular his *Parullat me gurë*,

Tirana 2003 (The Slogans in Stone), have been translated into French and Polish; the prolific **Diana Çuli** (b. 1951) from Tirana; **Mehmet Kraja** (b. 1952) from Ulqin; **Visar Zhiti** (b. 1952) of Lushnja, author of the novel *Perëndia mbrapsht dhe e dashura*, Tirana 2004 (The Backward Deity and the Mistress); **Zejnullah Rrahmani** (b. 1952) of Podujeva, an elegant stylist of modern Kosova literature, now living in Ottawa; **Bashkim Shehu** (b. 1955) now of Barcelona, who, as son of the purged communist leader Mehmet Shehu, spent many years in prison, and whose works have appeared in French and Spanish; **Kim Mehmeti** (b. 1955) of Skopje, a volume of whose works has appeared in German; **Preç Zogaj** (b. 1957) from the region of Lezha who in June 1991 became the first non-communist minister of culture; the late **Teodor Keko** (1958-2002); **Besnik Mustafaj** (b. 1958) from Bajram Curri who served as Albanian ambassador in Paris and whose works are known in France and, to an extent, in Germany and Italy; **Ridvan Dibra** (b. 1959) of Shkodra; **Lazër Stani** (b. 1959) from *Pult near Shkodra*; the talented **Mira Meksi** (b. 1960) from Tirana; **Elvira Dones** (b. 1960) now living in the United States, who is author of the successful and exceptionally frank novel Yjet nuk vishen kështu, Elbasan 2000 (Stars don't dress up like that) on the subject of Albanian prostitution abroad; the fascinating **Mimoza Ahmeti** (b. 1963) from Kruja; **Arian Leka** (b. 1966) from Durrës; **Agron Tufa** (b. 1967), author of the novel *Fabula Rasa*, Tirana 2004 (Fabula Rasa); **Virion Graçi** (b. 1968) of Gjirokastra; and **Ardian-Christian Kyçyku** (b. 1969) of Pogradec, now living in Bucharest.

If one were to ask what the main achievement of Albanian written culture has been over the last few decades, the reply would certainly be, "Poetry, here, there and everywhere!" Verse collections, until very recently, accounted for over fifty per cent of literary output in all the major centres of Albanian-language publishing: Tirana, Prishtina, Skopje, Shkodra and Tetova. Even under the harsh conditions of a free market economy in an underdeveloped region, Albanian poetry has managed to survive and maintain its dynamism. When impoverished and ill-educated Albanian emigrants and refugees gather in Western Europe or in North America in their often dingy and always smoke-filled clubs, it is more often than not that they come together for a poetry reading. It is here that the soul of the Albanian nation finds its expression. Readable Albanian prose is admittedly a recent phenomenon, and drama is still a very much neglected genre, but the Albanians have always opened their hearts spontaneously to lyrics.

Poetry has flourished since the generation of the modern classics in Albanian verse, characterized by Ismail Kadare, Fatos Arapi and Dritëro Agolli. Among contemporary poets whose works have been or are being published as books in English are: the late **Azem Shkreli** (1938-1997), **Ali Podrimja** (b. 1942), **Flora Brovina** (b. 1949), **Eqrem Basha** (b. 1948), all of those works have been published or are being published by Gjonlekaj Publishing in New York; **Visar Zhiti** (b. 1952), whose works are to appear on 30 January 2005 in a bilingual, AlbanianEnglish edition called The Condemned Apple by Green Integer in Los Angeles; and **Luljeta Lleshanaku** (b. 1968) from Elbasan, whose verse has appeared in English in the volume Fresco, New York 2002; but there are many others whose works would be enjoyed if properly translated. Among such contemporary poets of note, mention may be made in particular of: **Sabri Hamiti** (b. 1950) of Podujeva; **Gëzim Hajdari** (b. 1957) living in Italy, who publishes in Albanian and Italian; **Abdullah Konushevci** (b. 1958) of Prishtina; **Gazmend Krasniqi** (b. 1963) from Shkodra; **Flutura Açka** (b. 1966) from Elbasan; **Arian Leka** (b. 1966); **Agron Tufa** (b. 1967) from Sohodoll in Dibra; the late **Ilir Belliu** (1970-2002) from Korça; **Rudian Zekthi** (b. 1970) from Elbasan; **Rudi Erebara** (b. 1971) from Tirana, who lives in the United States; **Lindita Arapi** (b. 1972) now living in Cologne, Germany; **Gentian Çoçoli** (b. 1972) from Gjirokastra; **Romeo Çollaku** (b. 1973) from Saranda; **Lindita Ahmeti** (b. 1973) of Skopje; **Ervin Hatibi** (b. 1974) from Tirana; **Ledia Dushi** (b. 1978); **Ensard Telegrafi** (b. 1980) from Tirana; and **Parid Teferiçi**. The list is endless.

Modern Albanian literature, both in Albania and in Kosova, is now, for the first time, at liberty to evolve and go its own way. Closer contacts with the works of other literatures, albeit in often shabby translations, have given rise to some initial copying of styles and themes, but in the long run, such influence can only serve to enrich creative writing in Albanian itself.

Throughout the decades of the Hoxha dictatorship, and indeed up to the final months of Serb rule in Kosova, the border between the two halves of the Albanian nation was kept sealed by their respective rulers. Rare were those who crossed it without suffering political repercussions. The Berlin Wall between the two halves of Germany was, in comparison, a sieve. The result of this imposed separation was the rise of two very different Albanian cultures and two different Albanian literatures.

Since 1999, the two countries have been getting to know one another, and getting used to one another. Their citizens are now able to meet and mingle. It has not been easy for the population at large, and many misunderstandings have arisen, but the exchange of experience has proven particularly broadening and fruitful for Albanian writers on both sides of the border. For the first time, they have become members of one common literary culture, a culture which is now twice as large as and much more diverse than the smaller ones they had known.

The once barren and rocky landscape of Albanian culture is now unfettered and fertile. The tender plant of Albanian literature, whose stalks and roots have been torn out of the sparse soil so often over the course of history, is blossoming anew.

[Lecture given at the Bektashi Teqe and Center, Taylor, Michigan, United States, on 28 January 2005. First published in: Illyria, New York, no. 1416, 4-7 February 2005, S. 5; 1417, 8-10 February 2005, S. 5; 1418, 11-14 February 2005, S. 3, 5.]

Heart in an Aquarium

I have no forest
To set free
The creature of calm…

My heart
Wedged
In an aquarium
Among the withered leaves
And water…

The wind throbs…

I feel
The flight of things
On the run.

[*Zemra n'akuarium*, from the volume *Seancë dimnash* (Shkodra: Camaj-Pipa, 1999).

The Child

The child
Stood alone
In the meadow
Hidden
Behind the homes,
Half-asleep,
With brown eyes
Like the bark
Of a dead tree…

His face
Leaning
Between his shoulders.

[*Fmij*, from the volume *Seancë dimnash* (Shkodra: Camaj-Pipa, 1999).

Rain in the Dark

Life
Wearies within me
Sensing every night
The pulse 'neath my temples,
The husks of grain
Beating
Against the whites of my eyes.

I have lost
My tongue
Pond'ring on you…

Between my lips
Yesterday's stale air,
The male face
Of spring…

Tears sketched
On the wall
Have hanged
Themselves…

The assault of dusk
Has roasted my soul,
The only slaughtered meat
Unfit to eat.

[*Shi n'terr*, from the volume *Seancë dimnash* (Shkodra: Camaj-Pipa, 1999).

Time for Sleep

The heavens
Have draped
All things…

I've misplaced
All colours,
While staring
At the lake…

All people
Never really
Existed…

When I talk to myself,
Only I am.
Time for sleep…

I have lost the lake!

[*Koha e gjumit*, from the volume *Seancë dimnash* (Shkodra: Camaj-Pipa, 1999).

One

Darkness hovers
Above me..

Shooting off
Circles and points…

There is a void
Within the house
And without…

Light
Withers
Of its own…

[*Nji*, from the volume *Seancë dimnash* (Shkodra: Camaj-Pipa, 1999).

My Age

Age of annual
Solitude…

This house
Is made
Of roots
And rays…

Never
Do I summon
Solitude
By its name…

I smell
The fleeting fragrance
Of absence.

[*Mosha ime*, from the volume *Seancë dimnash* (Shkodra: Camaj-Pipa, 1999).

The Weather is Hot

The priests
Are the only link
Between drowing and heaven…

The saints
Strain their legs,
The nuns
Pierce
Their teardrops…

We've been left
Alone,
Now that
The spirit is no more…

And they say
It is
Summer.

[*Ban t'nxehtë*, from the volume *Seancë dimnash* (Shkodra: Camaj-Pipa, 1999).

Prison

Lambs and sheep
Can't be seen at night...

The man
Weeps alone,
Counting
In his soul
Drowned fields
At eventide...

I am used to
Absence...
Things that hover,
Become covert...

Prison
Is not only
Being locked up.

[*Burg*, from the volume *Seancë dimnash* (Shkodra: Camaj-Pipa, 1999).

Every... Night

Every night
I count the fields,
Delight in the rusty
Crop
That will never
Be reaped…

My body
Does not know
What it desires…

I stand there
Biting my nails,
My chapped hands crack
When touched.

[*Për...natë*, from the volume *Seancë dimnash* (Shkodra: Camaj-Pipa, 1999).

Still Life

Blood fills
The well in the courtyard...

The rain and I
Are Alone,
Locked
Within ourselves...
And we set forth...

Flowers
Have no feast days,
Rainbow
Hidden
In a box...

Still life:
Children
Belly-split
Are the faces of the moon
On earth.

[*Natyrë e vdekun*, from the volume *Seancë dimnash* (Shkodra: Cam-
aj-Pipa, 1999).

Nun

The eagles first appeared
On a night
Of deceptive lights…

In fear…

The voice of my dream
Floods
My ear,
Blood
Flows
Over my fingers…

To forget...

My head
An asylum
Of lonely beings…

I want to live
A winter
That lasts forever,
With a rooster crowing
In my head,
The death of the fowl
In my soul.

[*Murgeshë,* from the volume *Seancë dimnash* (Shkodra: Camaj-Pipa, 1999).

Blue

I sense
The vaporous being
Of Christ
Inside me,
The cheeks of saints
On my face...
With a dream on my lips
I dissolve into ecstasy…

The days
Are not written
By name…

The shadow of the Cross
Melts
Into a thousand little
Feathery banners
In my lap,
In my breast…

Everything
Holds
Its breath,
You are
A heap
Of Christmases…

The echoes
Stem from my head,
The noises resound
From the Vaults
Angels
In the Soul...

The things I love
Are so far
From Earth.

[*Blu*, from the volume *Seancë dimnash* (Shkodra: Camaj-Pipa, 1999).

Autumn Flower

I want to die
Under this
Autumn flower,
Shackled
In a glass of water...

In winter
I have
Comets in my eyes,
Fir trees in my hair...

We have been wounded
By the ash of the moon,
Barefoot love
'mongst beings.

Whoever died last night
Did not see
The arrow coming.

[*Lule vjeshte*, from the volume *Seancë dimnash* (Shkodra: Camaj-Pi-pa, 1999).

Change

The Time
Has come
That we be seen
Wrapped
In the shadow of Freedom...

I am human,
I long for the things
I do not possess...

Nothing
Is
Closer,
Or farther,
Than Earth...

I passed
Fruit
To the worms,
Lilies
To the larvae...

Perhaps
My heart
Is deformed
(and I don't know it).

[*Ndryshue*, from the volume *Seancë dimnash* (Shkodra: Camaj-Pipa, 1999).

31

Green Water

When I am grown
I will be
Small…

Green water,
The sweetest grass
In the world,
A field
of wandering
Fish…

In the skies
Nothing belongs
To me
Nor on earth;
In my head I hear
The bleating of lambs
On stone,
See colours
Stuck
To the seeds of my eyes.

[*Ujë i gjelbër*, from the volume *Seancë dimnash* (Shkodra: Camaj-Pipa, 1999).

My Freedom

A creature whitened
On the wall,
In love
With the contours
Of your shadow.

Beneath the moon…

I hear the voice
Appearing
Before my sight.
Nest of lights…

I am missing
The chords
Of unheard
Music.

Choking
On my dreams,
Handcuffed.

My freedom
Dwells in the mountains,
The eldest
Of the poisonous plants.

[*Liria ime*, from the volume *Seancë dimnash* (Shkodra: Camaj-Pipa, 1999).

Ledia Dushi

Born in 1978 in the northern Albanian town of Shkodra. She studied Albanian language and literature and she continued and finished her master's and doctoral studies in ethnology-folklore. She worked both as a journalist and in municipal government, where she was responsible for culture in Shkodra City Hall. Then she worked at the University of Beograd as a lecturer for Albanian language and literature. During the last year she worked as a lecturer at the European University of Tirana. She is also a translator from English, Italian and Spanish. She translated authors as Gabriele D'Annunzio, Cesare Pavese, Dylan Thomas, Jorge Luis Borges, Umberto Eco, Andrea Camilleri, Carlos Ruiz Zafon, Jane Austen, Hilary Mantel. Her well-received verse is written primarily in the dialect of Shkodra, gegë. It has been published in the volumes: Ave Maria bahet lot (Ave Maria Turns to Tears), Tirana 1997; Seancë dimnash (Winter's Session), Shkodra 1999; Me mujt me fjet me kthimin e shpendve (If I could sleep with the bird's return...), Tirana 2009 and a volume of her verse has also appeared in Italian, Tempo di pioggia (Rainy Weather), Prishtina 2000. Her poems are translated into German, Polish, French, Macedonian, Greek and Serbian.

Robert Elsie

Born on June 29, 1950 Vancouver, British Columbia, Canada, Elsie studied at the University of British Columbia, graduating in 1972 with a diploma in Classical Studies and Linguistics. In the following years, he continued his post-graduate studies at the Free University of Berlin, at the École Pratique des Hautes Étudesand at the University of Paris IV: Paris-Sorbonne, at the Dublin Institute for Advanced Studies, and at the University of Bonn, where he finished his doctorate on Linguistics and Celtic Studies in 1978 at the Linguistics Institute. From 1978 on, Elsie visited Albania several times with a group of students and professors from the University of Bonn. For several years, he also attended the International Seminar on Albanian Language, Literature and Culture, held in Pristina, Kosovo. From 1982 to 1987, he worked for the German Ministry of Foreign Affairs in Bonn, and from 2002 to 2013 for the International Criminal Tribunal for the former Yugoslavia in The Hague, in particular as an interpreter for several noted cases including the trial of Slobodan Milošević. Elsie's scholarly travels and interest in Albanian dialects brought him into contact with Albanians from Albania, Kosovo, Greece, Montenegro, Italy, Croatia, Bulgaria, Ukraine,Macedonia, and Turkey and made dozens of recordings of the Albanian language. As a translator Robert Elsie offered the reader "a selection of songs from the best known cycle of Albanian epic verse". Elsie during his lifetime authored many works of scholarship and had no unpublished work left for completion prior to his death.

www.ingramcontent.com/pod-product-compliance
Lightning Source LLC
Chambersburg PA
CBHW071802020426
42331CB00008B/2382